Praise for

FAR FROM ATLANTIS

"I have long been a fan of Raymond Luczak's writing, but *Far from Atlantis* moves in another stratosphere. In poems that shimmer with the harshness of a literally and figuratively cold childhood in Michigan's Upper Peninsula, deafness separates Luczak from the hearing-centric world; indeed, even from his own hearing family. Aching with memory and longing, with absence and connection, with what disappears and what can be recovered, including the bounty of mythical Atlantis, these richly imagined poems left me spellbound."

—Andrea Scarpino, author of *Once Upon Wing Lake*

"Prolific and talented poet Raymond Luczak has published another powerful collection, a lyric autobiography that draws on the myth-filled waters of his youth in Michigan's Upper Peninsula. These expertly controlled poems dive into the alienation, pain, and longing of being othered in an ableist world: 'There had to be a better planet where I didn't have to feel like an alien . . . I could touch the stars.' Luczak ultimately finds redemption through community: 'I had no idea I'd be waiting for the right supernova to shine.' From the watery depths of Lake Superior to the intergalactic travels of superheroes, these glorious poems shine strong."

—Kathryn Kysar, author of *Pretend the World* and *Dark Lake*

FAR FROM ATLANTIS

POETRY

Chlorophyll
Lunafly
once upon a twin
Bokeh Focus
A Babble of Objects
The Kiss of Walt Whitman Still on My Lips
How to Kill Poetry
Road Work Ahead
Mute
This Way to the Acorns
St. Michael's Fall

FICTION

Widower, 48, Seeks Husband
Compassion, Michigan
Flannelwood
The Last Deaf Club in America
The Kinda Fella I Am
Men with Their Hands

NONFICTION

A Quiet Foghorn: More Notes from a Deaf Gay Life
From Heart into Art: Interviews with Deaf and Hard of Hearing Artists
and Their Allies
Notes of a Deaf Gay Writer: 20 Years Later
Assembly Required: Notes from a Deaf Gay Life
Silence is a Four-Letter Word: On Art & Deafness

DRAMA

Whispers of a Savage Sort and Other Plays about the Deaf American Experience
Snooty: A Comedy

AS EDITOR

Lovejets: Queer Male Poets on 200 Years of Walt Whitman
QDA: A Queer Disability Anthology
Among the Leaves: Queer Male Poets on the Midwestern Experience
Eyes of Desire 2: A Deaf GLBT Reader
When I am Dead: The Writings of George M. Teegarden
Eyes of Desire: A Deaf Gay & Lesbian Reader

FAR FROM ATLANTIS

poems

RAYMOND LUCZAK

Gallaudet University Press
Washington, DC

Gallaudet University Press
gupress.gallaudet.edu

Gallaudet University Press is located on the
traditional territories of Nacotchtank and Piscataway.

Far from Atlantis: Poems
© 2023 Raymond Luczak

ISBN 978-1-954622-24-1 (paperback)
ISBN 978-1-954622-25-8 (ebook)

Library of Congress Cataloging-in-Publication Data
Library of Congress Cataloging-in-Publication Data

Names: Luczak, Raymond, 1965- author.
Title: Far from Atlantis : poems / Raymond Luczak.
Description: Washington, DC : Gallaudet University Press, [2023] | Summary:
    "Far from Atlantis is the latest collection of poetry by deaf author
    Raymond Luczak. In Far from Atlantis, Luczak makes use of traditional
    poetic forms to tell the stories of two vastly different worlds: the
    Upper Peninsula of Michigan and the fabled island of Atlantis"--
    Provided by publisher.
Identifiers: LCCN 2023013720 (print) | LCCN 2023013721 (ebook) | ISBN
    9781954622241 (paperback) | ISBN 9781954622258 (ebook)
Subjects: LCGFT: Poetry.
Classification: LCC PS3562.U2554 F37 2023 (print) | LCC PS3562.U2554
    (ebook) | DDC 811/.54--dc23/eng/20230330
LC record available at https://lccn.loc.gov/2023013720
LC ebook record available at https://lccn.loc.gov/2023013721

∞ This paper meets the requirements of ANSI/NISO Z39.48–1992 (Permanence of
Paper).

Cover image by Adam Kauwenberg-Marsnik
Cover design by Mona Z. Kraculdy

Cover description: Against a gray and overcast seascape in which there seems no
discernible horizon, a dull rust-colored rock formation island with a squat tree bejeweled
with orange leaves on top appears like a ship on a tranquil sea, its gentle waves the color
of brown coal. Above the island is the title FAR FROM ATLANTIS. Below the book's
title is the subtitle "poems." Far below on the cover is the author's name RAYMOND
LUCZAK.

for

Mary Nichols

Some of the poems in this collection include depictions of audism, ableism, and suicide. Readers who may be sensitive to these elements, please take note.

CONTENTS

IN IRONWOOD

IN ATLANTIS

YOUR BONNET
after Lucy Frances Fitzhigh Hooe (1827–1882)

1.

Up north the wind was your best friend,
but he never stayed around for long,
certainly never on Keweenaw Peninsula.
He whispered all sorts of things
you knew you shouldn't be thinking,
but there you listened, hesitating,
knowing how your sister Richardette
had warned you about soldiers daring
to look. When you bent down to ladle up
a cup of water from the lake,
no one knew how much fate you'd drink.
Oh, how no one knew at seventeen!

All you knew was how tired you were
of the loneliness swirling icy drafts
around the fingertip of Keweenaw Peninsula,
stiffer than your shoulders from butter churning.
You knew you weren't cut out for this life
huddled inside Fort Wilkins.

So when that stranger touched your hand
without saying another word,
you knew never to say another word.
You couldn't believe how a kiss could
shudder, exploding spasm after another.
You were soaking wet! Birds snickered
as you took off your bonnet and shook your hair
loose. The wind giggled at you.

Then you abruptly vanished.
Had the wind stolen you too?

2.

Whoever thought you'd left behind
your bonnet had a masterstroke moment
off the shore of the very lake
that was named after you.
From all the wild stories told around a fire,
they would've suspected a wolf
or even a bear still lurking in these parts
would attack you or wonder
if you'd crossed the road
for the choppy waves of Lake Superior
into the undersea world of suicides
whose dark blood turned into algae
that never quite came clean off the rocks
no matter how many times the waves scrubbed
them on the hottest summer day.

3.

More than a century
after your mysterious disappearance,
we were able to verify a few facts.

You visited Fort Wilkins at the northernmost
tip of Keweenaw Peninsula
during its first occupation. Your older sister
was married to First Lt. Daniel Ruggles,
who, twenty years later, would be the last Confederate
that John Wilkes Booth saw right before he died.

You lived there for only one year
before you married Chester B. White
four years later and birthed three children.
He died at the Benicia Barracks near San Francisco.
You applied for a widow's pension but were denied.

You lobbied for the next nine years
until Congress awarded you a monthly pension of $20.
By then you'd moved back to Fredericksburg, Virginia.
You died of cancer fifteen years later.
Fort Wilkins recently framed a copy of your death certificate,
the final inoculation against those stories.

4.

When I was ten, I camped off the shore
of the lake where you allegedly vanished.
Inside Fort Wilkins's main building,
my teacher and her husband smiled
at each other as I wandered
among the counter of plaques
detailing the various outcomes
you might've suffered. No one knew then.

Afterwards, I trailed behind my teacher,
a tentative fawn with his doe,
through the mottle of birch
flickering shards of white bouncing
off the lake's trampoline.
I didn't need my hearing aids:
My eyes could hear everything.
All I needed was to believe.

I wondered if she, too, would disappear.
I don't remember falling asleep in the tent,
but the shock of finding her still there,
scenting a waft of coffee off a small campfire,
was a relief. As it turned out,
I was the one who would disappear.

5.

Fort Wilkins is now a state park
where tourists idle among the buildings.
Snapping pictures with digital cameras
has become a thoughtless art,
a far journey's call from the days
when you had to sit still for years
trying not to blink at the cataracted lens,
searing a steely-eyed impatience
onto the daguerreotype plate.
But you weren't important enough to have
your picture saved for eternity.

Please let me call your name
so you can disappear again, this time for real,
leaving your bonnet in my hands,
clinging to the peripheral vision
of my memory. I am
still waiting, standing guard right here
on these shores where I've never left.

IN IRONWOOD

CURRENTS OF IRONWOOD

As a boy I climbed over the hill and down to Montreal River
where it burbled and flickered mosquitoes in late afternoons
when the sun was already departing from the trees
on the other side. The air soon turned cool
as I stared down at the twig-entangled water
where frogs propelled against the current.

The town where I grew up has lost its iron-ore current.
I don't see any kids playing down by the river.
Have they become afraid of its purified water,
or have they squandered perfect summer afternoons
on their smartphones? Don't they know that being cool
isn't what it's cracked up to be? I wonder if these trees

remember me as a boy at all. It's been said that trees
share a collective memory rather like a current
of electricity, their roots staying knit to spite the cool
and hot changes in the weather. Montreal River
is a reminder of ghosts wandering each afternoon;
after all, it has vast underground tributaries of water

into which a few mineshafts collapsed. Its waters
swallowed immigrant miners, stripping roots clean from trees,
yet the color of blood stained those dark afternoons.
The relentless greed for more electrified the current
to build another mine not too far from the river;
the grief for the lost miners was never allowed to cool.

Deeper and deeper into the earth where the air never cooled,
the miners thought of their loved ones drinking water,
doing homework, and making that night's meal. Montreal River,
being so polluted then, sludged along under the trees.
Sewage was dumped there. In those days, connecting currents
of electricity was a new concept. Mornings and afternoons

provided sufficient light. But at the end of each afternoon,
the miners felt the need to see more light. Cooled
by the breezes, they stood to watch the currents
slither unseen and rust-blooded in the murk of water.
They brushed away the flies buzzing about the trees
only to stare deeply back home into their childhood rivers.

My heart's still here. This river once whiled away entire afternoons
of my imagination, now lost to the cool breezes under the trees.
Currents still carry the boy I used to be along the Montreal River.

ODE TO THE NUNS

Sing me a song, oh you nuns who once
made a habit of viewing me a dunce
when I couldn't lipread you from the front row.
You *o*-ver-en-*un*-ci-at-ed to show
everyone how you could accommodate
a poor hearing-impaired soul in his state.

    My hearing aid harness
    underneath my shirt
    looked like a bra, a dress.

Sing me a song, oh you nuns in black,
glaring at the smirking boys in the back
who drew pictures mocking my ears.
I fought back with shuttering my tears,
never glancing back while I lipread.
I practiced my smiles until I was dead.

    The peach cords woven fine
    and upward from my body aids
    created a scapular all mine.

Sing me a song, oh you nuns in prayer,
heads bowed with curled bangs of your hair,
pufferies of cloud, as hymns to the Lord
struck another intricate chord.
During Masses you knelt unveiled
while I felt forever failed.

FANTASTIC ARCHAEOLOGY: HAIBUN
at St. Vincent de Paul Thrift Store, McLeod Avenue

Ladies older than time itself flitted among the islands of blouses and skirts clutching onto rickety hangers next to the land of salt-seared snow melted into puddles. They wore striped sleeveless shirts and teal cat-eyed glasses. They were powerful priestesses blessed with a magic marker and a gaggle of blank price tags punch-holed for stringing. They constantly blessed with a smile at anyone who opened the glass door to the wide cavern perfumed with the dust of time both bottled and unthrottled. The fluorescent rods above the sad shelves armored with mass-market paperbacks, cassette tapes in broken plastic cases, Scotch-taped board games with missing pieces, pancake stacks of 45s, baggies jowl-cheeked with marbles, boxes of thick *Reader's Digest* compendiums, and piles of *Fate* magazine, a monthly missive that free-willed through UFO abductions, the Bermuda Triangle, Uri Geller's spoon-bending, divining rods . . . For a nickel each, I was forever spellbound. They somehow sounded truer than the Bible, but could all these stories, smacking of scientific hocus-pocus, really be true? If I wanted to believe, I had to dig, just like I had with the glossy pages of my Baltimore Catechism book that I'd read during Mass, seeking answers from anywhere.

My hands, filled with soil
promising revelations:
only unclean truths.

NESSIE

Waves bobbing to and fro—pull back to reveal her—prehistoric profile—her neck sloped like a giraffe's—two flat bumps on her head—such quicksilver eyes.

Was that murky snapshot a lie?

Crowds flocked there, hoping for a show—of her dark green head—so they waited for her—holding ready guns and gaffs—but so much time on trial . . . on Loch Ness a long while—rain cold stormy clouds tired eyes—always thirsting for another carafe—cursing praying *please show*—more than waves a long stir—*please let us zoom in on her head—we must see her before we're dead*—scanning across each mile—our binoculars on her—hoping to catch her awakening to rise—from murky depths to glow—a shadow of giraffe—a perfectly focused photograph—a clear view of her head—her hump still as a floe—the clarity worth the while—such mystery in her eyes—such dreamers are we for her—the way we wait for her—ready to photograph.

Yet experts insist she is a lie—evidence not a shred!

Yet everyone monitors my imperfect ears in denial—I might as well go hide below—let them all worry feeling halved—from us monsters—let them all cry—when they catch us glow—at last in the sunset the waves of our lives left unsaid—

ENDLESSLY IN RIVERSIDE CEMETERY

Here in this village

the sun is horrible:

until the hiss of

around her throat,

let the crickets

alerting the dead

reunion. Music from

up like fog,

beside their fathers

Everyone

how this will end.

stuck in reverse,

humming and groaning

but yes oh yes

entire marriages

dawn, unraveling

bandying about.

of granite markers

Her snickers never stop

dark coils

long enough to

play their violins,

to yet another

their pasts rise

and the brides march

down the road.

in the audience knows

Their memories,

are heavy as organs,

not again,

again. Of course,

race toward

with accusations

return to their plots

separate beds.

to rot from their thoughts

Former soldiers,

caked around

lean against

Their voices

stratagems

gone right,

They never

the fate of buddies

tossed asunder.

sleep with their wives

next to them.

could understand

take a life

left inside them

Soldiers are forever

Husbands and wives

and sleep in their

They continue

of missed ripostes.

with splattered blood

their eyes,

the tombstones.

murmur war

gone wrong,

and gone what-if.

speculate

severed in half,

They never

though buried

Who else

what it took to

or how much war is

after peace?

damned with victory.

The widows sit

on the sidelines, making

small talk,

barely heard.

Loose tongues

have the power

to convict.

Those condemned

never return

to the blasted reunions

until the day

the righteous

are outnumbered

and then the cycle

of heaven and hell

starts again.

OUIJA

in November 1977

My chair stiffened me
trying to comprehend:

    the absence of Grandma.

The letters frowned in an arc.
The numbers stayed grim:

    the drawing of stillness.

The dining room table
rounded up whose spirits:

    the question of death.

Their breathing exhaled
shudders down my spine:

    the answer of silence.

The planchette awaited
my lonely touch.

A PRAYER TO URI GELLER

O can you grant me the telekinesis
to bend the spines of these boys always taunting
so they'd buckle from such maleficent pain,
their bodies mere spoons?

> On late-night television,
> your hands become a vision.

O can you lend your gift of telepathy
so I won't have to strain hard to read those lips,
my brothers and sisters gibbering away
around the kitchen?

> You are accused of fraud;
> yet people still applaud.

O can you divine me like the god you are,
communicating with extraterrestrials
53,000 light years away, so I
can rise up on high?

> Your backtrackings leave me
> confused. Who'd believe me?

O can anyone else save me from all this
gobbledygook of lips moving and faces
laughing as if I'm no longer a presence
misunderstanding?

ABDUCTIONS

Some summer nights I felt called to go outside.
With sequins of stars loosening in the sky,
I scanned all points from north to south, east to west.
    Twinkly as before,
the night didn't hint at a star that might turn
into a spacecraft, round as a plate aglow,
rainbow-colored, softly blinking and swooping
    down without a hum,
with not a wide window like on *Lost in Space*,
with not an underside door open-tonguing,
unleashing a green laser beam to zap me
    into submission.
There I'd be beamed up, strangely floating like a wisp
onto a table, feeling a rush of chill
across my body as their almond-downward
    eyes stayed unblinking.
The mucus-gray color of their skin would throb
eerily like a mood ring as they come close,
their narrow shoulders and small bodies would seem
    improbably frail
to support their enormous heads. But their eyes:
not a flicker of emotion or question,
just like how my doctor gazed at me before
    the anesthesia
kicked in. His eyes hovered above the white mask.
He asked how I was feeling, but I didn't
know this. I couldn't lipread through his fabric.
    His masked attendants
hovered nearby as I tried to resist the
urge to fall asleep. I'd spotted the trays of
surgical instruments shiny and ready
    as if for dinner.
He was to probe my right ear and see if he
could make it hear better. No one explained
just what would be done to me on that morning.

I had to trust him
totally like how Mom trusted our quiet priest,
Father Frank, who was impossible to read
on the lips; his Sunday babble made no sense.
        I lay white-sheeted,
feeling slightly chilled, as if the aliens
had entered the operating room as ghosts,
hovering as my mind's ear caught the static
        from their own language;
they seemed to be debating whether I should
be taken along to wherever they lived ...
Then I woke up to find Mom smiling,
        asking how I felt.
Not long after, when I became more alert,
my doctor anxiously smiled as I put in
my earmold to see if I could detect a
        change in my hearing.
None at all. My audiologist confirmed
it was still the same. That winter night I looked
up to the stars, yearning for the aliens
        to take me away.
There had to be a better planet where I
didn't have to feel like an alien, mute
with the ache for communication so clear
        I could touch the stars.

THE SIX MILLION DOLLAR DEAF BOY

After being abducted by aliens and left incoherent
in the woods across the street, the government

would quietly whisk me away into a secret hospital
where machine parts would be grafted, little by little,

onto my nonfunctioning body parts. Now bionic,
I would hear the quietest of sounds. Gone ultrasonic,

I would jot down hushed conversations
and stave off the threat of war from other nations.

I would fend off would-be assassins plotting
to kill President Carter and leave them rotting.

I would run tirelessly from Ironwood to Houghton,
never soaking any of my shirts, made of cotton,

over a mere 120 miles away
under an hour, zipping up the two-lane highway

just to see my best friend Todd and say hello.
I'd wear a headlight, sprinting like a whizzing glow,

as my bionic eyes would infrared deep into the trees
where Bigfoot would dare venture out of mystery

to forage for food only at night so he'd never get shot.
I would run beside Steve Austin and never feel fraught

with danger as he was my new father.
Protecting me wouldn't be a bother,

but evil men always kidnapped me, not knowing
of my abilities. My leaps would be mind-blowing

to all but me. Landing on the street 100 feet below
would be easy. My kidnappers would be abysmally slow,

trying to hurry down the escape stairs
while I'd leap up again through the air

atop another building. I'd survey the skyline
and calculate just where I could find

my new dad dashing through the streets,
zeroing onto the location of my heartbeat.

He'd find my kidnappers cursing again
to kill me. They'd hear a click, and then

my dad would kick open the iron door
with such force that they were floored,

but I wouldn't be. "Come on," he'd say.
"Let's go." Together we'd run far away

to a home where hearing perfectly
wasn't a requirement to be part of a family.

A BRIGHT GREEN

after Lou Ferrigno playing the Incredible Hulk (1977–1982)

With not a single sound,
shadows fall in the lab.
Would he be caught and stabbed?
Would his secret be found?

He's perfected his smile,
trying so hard to hide
the loneliness inside.
But sometimes his guile,

too long suppressed, can tear
apart his white lab coat.
His rage needs time to gloat
and toss anyone near.

How I'd longed to turn green
each time those boys turned mean.

LUCAN

after Kevin Brophy playing the eponymous character (1977–1978)

Atop a scrawny hill,
sprawled on his back
while surrounded by men
full of ugliness as
the sky looked down
a familiar trill
from the days when he grew
up a boy among the wolves,
he felt again the call,
a throb of yellow
glowing like neon
from inside his eyes,
a jolt of strength
from his childhood
pulsing from the trees,
his limbs suddenly pistoning
his captors away,
a nuclear blast of rage
that powered him
to run, run, *run*
into the woods he so loved
until he was Wolfen
again, closer to what
he was destined to be,
and far from those
who kept trying to corral him,
control his every movement
until he was absolutely
normal in every which way.
I wanted to say, "Lucan,
I've got these hearing aids.
They still treat me like
a wild animal."

BUCK ROGERS IN THE 25TH CENTURY

after Gil Gerard playing the eponymous character (1979–1981)

In those days of no closed captions, I barely understood
a word of dialogue zipping between Buck and Wilma
as they hopped in and out of makeshift jets
that didn't seem to require much power to blast off
into outer space without a single rumble.

Enemy jets zipped around them, turning into targets
blinking on Buck and Wilma's low-resolution screens
on their dashboards before they pressed a button,
not even glancing behind at the explosions
firing forth into nothingness among the stars.

The more I watched the show, the more I had to wonder
just how it was possible for anyone to survive
in space if their glass tops didn't seem to have a tight fit.
They wore fairly thin uniforms that didn't need
to screw on those glass domed helmets.

How much room did their slim jets have for those missiles
that seemed automatically stockpiled before taking off again?
I lost count. They didn't seem worried about running low
on fuel either. I pondered how their hairstyles could've stayed
the same for five centuries. What about their near-disco makeup?

I watched the show anyway. Gil Gerard was virile
in the same way I hadn't quite grasped either with Lee Majors
running in slo-mo as the Six Million Dollar Man.
Not knowing the existence of subtitles, I wanted
to read sentences gliding out of Mr. Gerard's mouth

in such moments when he climbed onto the wing of
his jet, glancing back with a grin at me, saying, "Hey,
buddy. I could use some help. You can hop in the back."

Together we would race among the stars,
spinning upside down and sideways, all the while

blasting one enemy target after another, not realizing
that one day very soon I would experience my first
explosion, shattering the smallness of my universe
in the starless inner space far from any man,
not quite understanding the dialogue of my growing body.

YEARS BEFORE THE FLOOD

Just before my voice broke into manhood,
I stood in the basement with my mother.
She had been hanging clothes
fresh from the washer. She pointed to my armpits
and pinched her nose with a look of disgust.
My mother said:
                    "You smell."

I wanted to die. I wanted to
evaporate into the sweetest of perfumes—
lilacs, apple blossoms, roses.
I wanted to be a stowaway from a ship having sunk
just off the island of Atlantis, miraculously overlooked
by radar and satellite, just like the island of Themyscira.

Instead I saw in my mother's eyes not a normal person
reflected back like her other eight children. A dodo bird
long overdue for extinction, I had thingamabobs
plugged into the ironclad ship of my head.
If I dared to unplug my ears, my bottled pain
would flood the basement. She would surely drown.
I would dolphin free. In water I would not smell.

THE DEAF BOY FROM ATLANTIS

after Patrick Duffy playing the Man from Atlantis (1977–1978)

I was all legs and bones when you appeared
covered with kelp on TV. A storm had appeared,

flinging you from the bottom of the sea
onto the shore. A father and son appeared

and called for help. You found it difficult to breathe
there in the hospital. Yet Dr. Elizabeth Merrill appeared

to figure out what needed to be done. You were
brought back to the ocean, where you finally appeared

revived with your webbed feet and hands. Then
the phrase LAST CITIZEN OF ATLANTIS ????? appeared

on the computer screen. You glanced at the people
and their strange customs. Confused, you appeared

to everyone, but you kept silent, not yet speaking.
You had to get out when an open window appeared

in the government building where you were kept.
You didn't know you had to pause when cars appeared

driving down the street, and you ended stuck in a phone booth,
frantic that you couldn't open its door. A young boy appeared,

pushing open to let you out. You wandered lost, dazed
at this foreign world opening up. Dr. Merrill appeared

just in time to find you full of enigmatic wonder.
You eventually learned to speak English and appeared

to learn gradually the odd gesture of shaking hands
with each new acquaintance. Yet you still appeared

to ache for water. There, you bobbed forward,
your hands at your sides. Your bright green irises appeared

to glow in the water. The deeper you swam past
scuba divers, the more alive you appeared,

not worrying at all whether you'd run out of oxygen.
Your lungs were enclosed in a chest that appeared

perfectly sculpted with its supple pectorals.
You were nothing like me as I appeared

barely a skeleton. But I knew we could be friends
because of how strange the hearing world appeared

to the two of us. Perhaps I'd forgotten how to swim
and I was destined to remember when you reappeared.

IN ATLANTIS

ISLAND BABY

Nails half-covered pearls.
Nose a tender snout, a fin.

Toes squiggly agates.
Head a smoothed coconut.

Arms luminescent sponges.
Hair a bare stream among reefs.

Eyes undulant octopuses.
Neck a tortoise's lengthening.

Legs dangling branches:
This happy dolphin will thrive.

Hadn't anyone around the kitchen table thought
  to see if I was following their banter all right?

The darkness surrounding the stars in the cold snap
  soothed my eyes into cooling my rage.

Was there a planet better than this one out there?
  Please Superman me to where I can be reborn.

AMPHITRITE

I never wanted to mother.
My veins throbbed brine.
My dolphins were best friends.
My eyes could spear far
into the depths and hear
the soft movements
of creatures whose names
I never needed to learn.
My skin had a hint
of blue-gray waxiness.
I liked the way it breathed
memory and warmth
when I shimmied down
under the waves. The sky
above was just bad weather.
The undercurrents breezed
through my hair
whenever it thundered,
flipping the ships above.
Looking up at the flickers
of fire and silhouettes
of sailors drifting away
in silence, I wondered
why anyone would want land.
I always walked funny.

The fluidity of goldfish
    swept through me,
my body a tank of envy.
        How could they not fear
the algae of death
        each time I tried to swim?

One night I tripped over
a fallen coconut on the shore.
Poseidon sat up among
his buddies still carousing.
His voice, a god's timbre,
demanded that I reveal my face.
I stumbled off into the waves.
Then one sea creature after another
chortled his same message: *Now*.
I slipped away into the mountains.
A dripping coldness chilled me.
Emaciated, I tried to end my life
by diving right into the rocks
at the bottom of a waterfall.
Instead I was carried home
back to the sea. Dolphins click-
clicked perhaps it was time to marry.
I blanked out on my wedding night.
I hated his body, reeking of wine
and sweat and musk and grunt.
I kept my distance afterward.
A small army of dolphins clustered
around me each time he swum by.
I did not want to be his island.
When he watched our baby
dolphins sliding out from me
into the waves, he sobbed.
I still would not mother.

My hearing aids were supposed
    to lifejacket me to safety
whenever the sea of hearing babble
    capsized my spirits.
Instead I spent raft-days seeking
    my lost compass.

THE CLAIRVOYANT

When I sleep, I don't dream.
Inside me the dark sky
shows no stars where I fly
without worry or scheme.

But last night the moon stirred
my heart awake with shouts— *words*

    forgetting hereabouts—
      regretting what I'd heard— *birds*
    my floor of stone shaking—
      planks of my table splitting— *quitting*
    crows cawing and flitting—
      mortared bricks breaking— *shaking*

Outside a shot of flame
soon became a river

of lava and sulfur   *—that smell—*
pouring from whence it came,
its bubbles a deathly hiss
among those trapped too soon.   *—such hell—*

The lava filled the lagoons
burning all to abyss.

Edgar Cayce would reincarnate in me
    with a flowering of my ESP,
my homeopathic recipes curing their past lives,
    my warnings the purest karma,

my answers detailing future traumas,
    until I outpredicted Jeane Dixon.

On wings I felt guided
with stars weighted on me
as I looked to the sea
slapping ships lopsided,
and doomed to crack and sink.

Screams of horror and pain
on the streets begged for rain
to stop the lava's brink.

Horror sputtered in gasps
as the temple's columns
buckled to the bottom.
No one could ever grasp
this vision swarming in,
blood filling my third eye.
Staggered, I couldn't cry.

Then I awoke in a spin:

the morning sun swept in,
a crisp painting of gold,
a sudden joy to behold.

My room hadn't fallen.
Nothing had shattered.
I wept from being spared.

But what could I predict of my own life
to come? All I knew was
an older deaf man who was a high school dropout
and washed dishes for Holiday Inn.

Would I end up just like him, a freak
awash in the suds of absence?

But the nightmare still blared
in my eyes: such tattered
visions of sediment
gone molten made me sound
quite mad. I felt stone-ground
by their cold sentiment.

With fine days glistening,   { *breathe breathe breathe* }
no one is listening.   { *breathe breathe breathe* }

Sitting at the dinner table with my siblings
    constantly warring for each other's attention,
they often forgot a deaf boy was there.
    I asked the stars to teach me how to invisible myself.

Eating alone amidst their babble, I imagined a future
    in which they drowned in their own hearing.

HERMES

On the days when I'm bored
I swoop down in disguise,

brandishing my fine sword,
and strut around with lies

of having conquered Troy
and having kissed Helen.

It's a well-practiced ploy
to drink wine, eat melon,

and scope who else I can
fleece out of pride and coins

quickly lest I get banned.
Until then I ply loins

like strings on a lyre.
Nothing like teasing fire.

At eleven, I never grasped those wavelengths
    of love pulsating from the radio.

Why would a man want to kiss a woman?
    Why would a woman want to die for her man?

Nobody wanted me as a friend.
    Those songs had to be sung by liars.

THE MERMAID

Her long hair undulates with her shoulders
  as she plunges in like a sword for one more swallow
of peace. She can still smolder
  as if the ocean can't extinguish and hold her;
she is all fire and fury inside her body's hollow.
  Her long hair undulates with her shoulders
as she rises, breaking surface among the boulders.
  Her eyes, like my mistresses, dare me to follow
in war. She can still smolder
  afar even late at night when stars, far older
and wiser than all, command her to stay low,
  her long hair undulating with her shoulders
twinkling. I ache to dive into the dark and hold her,
  but my healer says I've become too sallow
from war. She can still smolder
  against my body if she desires, but I'm too old. Her
face—no, she'd see my liver spots turned yellow.
  Her long hair undulates with her shoulders
for peace. She can still smolder.

The long finger of breakwater
    that gate-kept the rowdy Lake Superior
from overwhelming the Black River Harbor
    always beckoned me closer. Surely one day
I would slip amidst leaping from one jagged boulder
    to another into the teeth of the great gray beast.

THE SERPENT

Sailors knew better than go to the ocean's edge.
No one had ever returned.

Past the horizon, a squiggle of scales
flashed white glints in the sun.

Stories swirled about the beast sliming
under the strangely still waves.

It was longer than any island.
It coiled around the largest ships with length to spare.

Its scales were wider than any ship's sail.
Its edges were sharper than swords.

Its fangs were twice as tall as the tallest man.
Its tips never fractured when chomping into a blue whale.

Its eyes yellowed more than the sun in a clear sky.
Its nostrils blasted jolts of fire at ships.

Even if the sailors managed to escape and swim away,
days of no food and no rest in water roasted them in the sun.

Nobody knows what's out there.
This is why we campfire stories.

Leaning into Montreal River at Norrie Park,
*   I loved watching the tadpoles*

swimming in circles, as if caged
*   by the tall grasses holding firm in the water.*

They would one day become frogs,
*   leaping away to escape the monster of me.*

CHRYSUS

Nobody talks about me anymore.
Not even a footnote.
Everybody's even forgotten
about Theia, my legendary mama.
When she was having those problems
with her ex-boyfriend Mars,
she told me to take over gold.
Mars got really upset
because he wanted to run gold
for himself. There was nothing
he could do except to sputter
out orichalcum, an inferior alloy
of gold that rusted after a few years.
The metal became a joke in Atlantis.
Soldiers had to keep painting
over the walls of orichalcum
to prevent chipping into the waves.
Anyway, Mama said to keep your pet
ram away from all the gods.
Hide him in a cave somewhere.
That was a real tough ask.
How I loved that little feisty boy
Chrysomallos. Yes, I did name him
a bit after myself. I'd seen how
no one paid me much attention.

I had read stories about animal
    mothers rejecting their offspring

soon after their birth, leaving
    them to fend for themselves.

In the woods, I wondered if I was
    an abandoned animal in disguise.

I was just a plain girl. No marriage
prospects, really. I couldn't compete
with all those nymphs. I figured
I might as well mother a cute baby sheep.
No one in the herd wanted Chryso.
Even his mother didn't want him.
Chryso smelled different. And yellow.
And he had wings! Very odd.
He followed me everywhere.
The moment of his sprouting wings,
I will never forget. He leaped
from boulder to boulder, his wings
flapping, trying to figure out
the grace of catching wind to fly.
The moment he did, well,
his coat began to change color.
It was the radiance of the sun
but with a spangle of metal.
Mom went outta her mind
when she first saw him like that.
Don't you realize this wool is gold?
She nearly screamed to the skies.
But Chryso would not go anywhere
without me. All the gods swooped
down, trying to take him away,
but rams are hell to break.
Much tougher than wild horses.
Chryso followed me but only

The classroom was a zoo.
  Each of us was chained to our desks.

We could not roam at all.
  Our zookeepers wore rosaries,

the combination lock to our freedom.
  I was always the last one kept behind.

up to a point. I couldn't imagine
him sitting docilely in the cave
like Mama wanted. He loved to hover
above the herd, spitting vile amounts
all over his mother's coat so her wool
would be yucky and worthless.
Long story short, a few king's soldiers
kidnapped me and tied me up
on a mighty horse. Chryso followed me
into a grove reined in by fences
all around. He was chained
to the thickest olive tree in the middle.
I was bound with ropes to a nearby tree.
The soldiers shadowed my neck
with their poisoned arrows. Chryso
stood still while they sheared off
wool around his magnificent wings.
They didn't dare touch his feathers.
He was that big. Fury churned in his eyes,
but he tremored still. I knew
he wouldn't stay chained for long.
Of course, the king had to place
a few of his fire-spewing bulls
to guard the gates. Then that jerk,
so full of himself, had to barge in
with his argonauts once they sprung
their arrows into the bulls' eyes.
They ignored me when they hacked

Standing by the brick wall, I wondered
if I had exhibited the markings

of an exotic creature, waiting to be
photographed by gawkers

discreetly looking at me, nudging
each other, Just look at it!

at the chains holding Chryso back.
I had to chuckle when I saw how still
he'd stood while the sweaty soldiers,
euphoric over the biggest kill of their lives,
hammered away at the links. That boy
sure knew how to wait. Once freed, he ran
off to fly over the fence and disappeared.
I never saw him again. His golden fleece,
which no one had yet scoured before
spinning into threads, still hung
like banners around the big olive tree.
Like madmen, they climbed the tree,
stuffed all the fleece into a bag,
and ran off on their horses.
They didn't think to free me.
Luckily, a few goats wandered in
and found my wrist ropes tasty.
All those humans are dead. I'm not.
I don't know where Mama lives now.
I hear stories about her all the time,
but I never know if any of them are true.
Who cares about Atlantis these days?
All the gods have gone into hiding.
Well, anyway, look at this cute little cape
floating off my shoulders. So pretty
when it shimmers yellow in the sun,
and so light! I love how it moves
with the wind, always waving hello
to my hair saying goodbye.

Maybe I was never a wild animal,
*   but a bird who had needed to molt*

his feathers of ear-burning shame
*   and pimply awkwardness.*

I prayed to disappear. Time has blessed me
*   with these hands, the purest gold.*

THE ARCHER

My father was an archer of acclaim.
When he pulled his string and flexed his bow,
he squinted his good eye and tilted so
his supple shoulders stayed outside his aim,

targeting a fox, nibbling unaware,
before his arrow punctured its slim neck
and nailed it to the tree as if a peck.
I pulled out the arrowhead, almost clear

of blood. He beamed down at me and said,
One day you'll perfect your zinging-the-string
so your arrow can sing it anything
you hear. Just practice till your arms feel dead.

My sapling arms soon matured into trunks.
I'd already learned how to whittle bows;
I'd long practiced the art of letting go
until I could close my eyes and hit plunk.

By then I'd explored the southeast forest
and spotted a few unicorns sleeping.
Their secret place was mine for safekeeping;
I loved watching them snuggle in their midst.

Hiding in the wilds across the street, I crouched
low behind the tall grasses, hoping to catch

the rarest sight of a woodpecker pecking
on a tree trunk with the rifle of my eyes.

I would shoot the bird into the amber cradle
of memory to telegraph in my dreams.

Their horns spiraled as if made of pearl-jade
yet iridescent as moon-lit river.
Their white manes rarely gave a quiver
as they nosed together in the low glade.

When they awoke, their eyes were of deep brown,
the very color of the richest loam
that enabled the vines of grape to roam.
The unicorns left behind a deep crown

among the grasses. I dreamed of snatching
a foal and taming him so we'd impale
prey with horn and arrow. The size and scale
of our doubled talents could make catching

buffalo and panthers profitable
on an island where we breathed and ate fish.
How novel it'd be to serve a meat dish!
My sudden wealth would make affordable

a palace for my parents, and I'd live
simply with my loving wife and children.
The problem was, I had no such kindred.
Many women had made my heart misgive,

but one in particular gave me hope.
Airla wasn't the loveliest of all
but her coy glances made me feel quite tall.
I felt less of a bitter misanthrope.

The hormones of wildness broke free
  from the zoo of my gangly body.

I didn't understand why I was developing,
  only that I secretly crushed on this one boy

in class. I wanted to write him notes,
  caging him into my heart.

Her hair, black as tar, cascaded off her
shoulders like waterfalls down to her waist.
I felt an impudent blush in my face.
I knew that for marriage to occur,

I'd need to demonstrate wealth or some skill
that would contribute to food and shelter.
When Iason returned, a thick welter
of emotion swelled. He bragged how he'd killed

and persuaded her that they should marry?
When he'd left, he wasn't much of a man
but as a soldier, he had a game plan.
I knew I couldn't afford to tarry,

not when he'd trained in Sparta and kept score
killing traitors in Helen of Troy's name.
That I knew unicorns spread like a flame,
and then a group of archers showed up for

proof of their location in the grasses.
They jabbed me in my chest, saying, *Liar.*
Iason smirked at how I'd lit afire
in my cheeks as he swept our chalices

off the feasting table. *Yeah, tomorrow.*
That night Airla sat next to me and smiled.
I felt giddy with my heart beating wild,
but that night I felt a yawning sorrow

But this one boy always darted
    looks of ice at me each time.

I ached to sit next to him at lunch,
    his popularity glowing on me,

at least enough to shine back
    to melt the ice of disgust in his eyes.

envelop me as in a heavy mist,
as if their sleeping glade had disappeared.
No doubt warned, the unicorns would've cleared.
I thought again of how I should insist,

as I led the way, that I'd only lied.
Once there, though, the men gasped upon seeing
the unicorns sleeping, breathing, being.
The men quietly slid bows off their sides,

their shoulders slinking back for that ping.
Their gray arrowheads flinted in the sun
as they prepared to take aim as if one
Medusa ready for the snarling.

I leaped behind them onto a boulder.
I quickly speared into each of the men's
hearts and backs. No, they couldn't be my friends!
Growling, they twisted and turned their shoulders

around to zing me, but I'd quickly run
deep into the familiar trees and climbed
up where I surveyed for odd movements, primed
with my arrow to kill another one.

The moonless night, filled with its sounds, felt long.
By morning the vultures had descended,
their beaks picking clean the flesh distended.
I buried their bones. I had to fake strong

Winters in the Upper Peninsula were nothing
compared to the growing hypothermia

enveloping my unwritten love notes
that my heart had yet to ink.

How I wanted to boil my soul just so
that I wouldn't have any tears left.

when I returned with news of the dead.
Naturally they hunted for remains
of their loved ones, but it was all in vain.
Today I marry Airla. I still dread

the moment when the gods break the sky
to strike me dead with thunder and lightning,
my dishonest soul too frightening.
Oh, how I rue the day I learned to lie!

I'm still standing, but I've already died.
What will I teach my children with my bow?
Isn't it better to leave such prey just so?
Truth has pierced a gaping hole in my hide.

I hear that he's recently retired in Vegas.
    How had he gambled his life away?

I search for him online, a desert of so few
    images. His dimples are still there.

The oasis of my secret ache for him
    has long since evaporated. I am wind.

CARYATIDS

We stand together, sisters of the porch,
our bodies remembering the raw scorch
of chisel hammering away
our tender marble to display
how we held the weight
of our hips, the plait
of hair down
to our gowns,
until we
stood free,
embraced by sun.
But they weren't done
sheathing us in cloth and rope
as men dragged up the slope.
Then we were tilted up and forward,
pushed and aligned as ordered.
This took them a few days.
No one held us in praise
of our uniform bevy.
They complained how heavy
we were. If we were their mothers,
they'd have treated us like feathers,
certainly not this beam
squelching our dreams.
Each night on this damn porch
we await the flicker of torch.

In the entrance of the Ironwood Memorial Building,
a bronze doughboy statue perched forward,

holding a rifle down in his right hand
while his left hand reached out to grasp.

Ignoring the look of horror in his eyes,
I swung from that arm each time I visited.

POSEIDON
(Or: On Why He Stopped Creating Islands)

I swept my trident across
the sea until palm
trees and moss
arose with mountain and sand.
Once all became calm,
the new land
attracted men drunk on force,
having tired of alms
as recourse,
dreaming of power in hand,
women sweet as balm,
being fanned
in the shade as they wined, ruled
with orders to calm
those unschooled
in patience by tying them
up below a palm's
shady hem
where people flung coconuts
till death became balm
for bruised guts.

Ghost bodies floated
*   like driftwood across Lake Superior,*

their remaining threads of vein
*   quartzing into agate,*

still teeth-hungry for more blood
*   each time I barefooted into the waves.*

ORICHALCUM

But oh how little you know of us ghosts already rising:

late at night you so-called soldiers

will keep hearing us the dead

our endless waves

our silences trying to float

up our voices

rising in prayer and bobbing

out of the crimson

spilling and spreading

the color of your hatred

rusted in the hot sun

seeping out of your pores

we ghosts will lament

louder than night

icing the moon

in your winter veins

Kneeling Saturdays before Father Hollenbach,
I confessed my jewel-tiny sins.

I wondered if he ever heard them boys
confess how they'd slivered me.

I sought a diamond of compassion afterward.
His face remained a shield.

cursing you and your sons

oh you big fool gods

will pretend this new agony

sharp gasps of pain

didn't come from us

you all will turn into beasts

babbling incoherently

such madness in foment

no one will believe our voices

in your heads padlocked

and chained to our memory

inked in blood and silhouette

welcome to your own hades

How I wanted the gumption to brandish
a sword, rattle his shield:

a new language of sounds from this boy
learning to pierce such condescensions

with a mere glance, knowing that one day
the meek would inherit the earth.

NIP IN THE AIR

The color of dreaming in the night air
changes when death comes without fanfare.
The panther doesn't move as it stares
into the darkness from the perch of its lair.
Coconuts knocking each other err
enough to drop on turtles sleeping there.
Wild dogs nestle together to share
warmth without a single care.
Owls await, with their ears sharp aware,
mice scurrying here and there.
Far down below stallions and mares,
flicking their tails, sleep in pairs.
A snake knots a noose to ensnare
the innocent brown hare.
The moon, shimmering its glare
on the sea, dissipates everywhere.

Grandma's house began to bottle up with water
    from the leaking roof in the attic.

It had dribbled down the stairs next to the fridge.
    I hadn't noticed the puddles at first.

I looked for a bucket, a mop, then another bucket.
    I pell-melled back and forth to the sink.

But the water! Its benignity undertowed
    the snake of patience and death.

None of the doors to outside would open.
    I ran around, trying all the windows on the first floor.

People driving past never noticed the boy
    pounding on the glass, screaming.

Tonight my love has ended our affair.

She wept goodbye in my hair and left me standing on top of my
stairs as her husband's eyes warned, *Beware.*

As she swept past him, his eyes dared me to go fight him in the
square where pear blossoms sighed in the air.

When I closed my door, he blared a snort, flinging me a shroud of
shame to wear.

I'll surely grow beastly as a bear, starving of love's hunger in my lair!
How can I survive this glare of my wrong? I am a poor man's heir.

Of my love to her, I swear, I shall hold no other spare.

I ran back to the kitchen.
  The pots and pans were drifting.

   The metal-edged table spun slowly.
     The chairs bobbed as if ducklings.

      The fridge tilted sideways,
        twisting out boats of butter and milk.

        I finger-climbed along the wall,
          my body rising up to the ceiling.

          I paddled toward the stairs,
            a growing waterfall with no sheen.

            My feet felt so good to landfall on the steps.
              I clung to the handrails for the attic.

Slithering upward from down there,
      the first quiet tremor travels to where
the animals sleep. It feels like a warning blare.
      The unicorns angle their horns to stare.
Where to go? The island is in the middle of nowhere;
      not much land. They would all get ensnared
even without soldiers rushing everywhere
      to organize panicky humans for warfare.
Dogs leap up and growl with teeth bared.
      Birds unleash a torrent of cries midair.
Whinnies ricochet among stallions and mares,
      shaking their heads against stable walls to tear
off for a mad dash across the square.
      Panthers climb palm trees like stairs
and ponder whether they should care.
      The next tremor can no creature forbear.

[Up in Grandma's attic, Mom pointed out where she used to sleep. An attic window: too small for the dreams she must have had. A lonely twin-size bed: she was the youngest child, an accident. A layered cake of wool blankets: scant heat fled the chimney outside her room. A glass of water: in winter the glass would have iced overnight. A naked lightbulb hanging from the ceiling: the parchment of story in light, the ache for story at night. This house suddenly felt haunted when Grandma died. A new chill crept upward from my feet to my head: Did ghosts really exist? All those library books had said so. Ghosts knew they had died but hadn't wanted to leave just yet. I kept glancing at the stairs beside the stove. Maybe she'd paused up there, realizing she wasn't quite ready to depart. Would I ever catch her gauzy face?]

Nights ashore are without compare:
    a gentle breeze is a prayer
        answered whenever I despair
            of another sleepless nightmare.

Walking along the sea so fair,
    I collect tears in my hands and stare
        until nothing left to share.

A chill suddenly whiplashes where
    my heart has felt torn bare.
        Have I imagined it elsewhere?

This unexpected nip in the air,
    sharp and nasty, is a scare.
        But the skies reveal nothing rare;
            there is no comet flare.

Yet fate has doomed me to nowhere:
    this feeling I cannot air.

The flooding rising upstairs poured into Mom's bedroom.
The water became fingers of ice around my feet.
        The tiny window was a glassed Fort Knox.
        There was no chair for me to throw and shatter its pane.
The water pushed me off my feet. Mom's bedframe banged against the ceiling.
No air left. My body was a writhing mass of prayers.
        In the blue-green depths, I sensed a presence,
        an invisible pulse of light.

Was I about to enter the tunnel
where my dead beloveds would embrace me?
        I opened my eyes for the last time.
        A radiance of long white hair

spreading outward like the sun
glimmered, her hands waving me to go back.
        I awoke, dry, to find a breadcrumb trail of shiny pennies home.

BEYOND IRONWOOD

———————

STANDING BEFORE LAKE SUPERIOR

No matter how bright the blue sky is,
the sun always becomes gray on the waves,
its swaying membrane of transparency
a pale nothing like the skin that enclosed
its jangly mass of muscle, veins, and nerves
just enough for it to swim without fear.

Yet it aches for a mouth-hole pried open,
a kiss rushing to flood the rivulets
of lung trapped madly inside the rib cage
until the body stiffens into a dream
among chunky logs softened by wind, sun,
and storm. Such tales are forever bottled.

The mouth is the gateway to everything,
including the elegies yet to sing.

THE ARCHANGEL MICHAEL

In my dreams he stood as tall as my family's church.
His feet were as big as the cars parked across the street.
The hems of his robe picked up bits of rust and birch.

His granite-colored wings were wide as a city block.
His eyes were constantly scanning the horizon.
I prayed for strength against names thrown like rocks,

but no one ever responded. I left town for good.
My family's church was eventually dismantled.
Who knew that money could be stronger than blood?

He is no longer standing proudly above the skyline.
The entire town has become a crime scene:
his body, when felled, was too big to chalk in outline.

The ghost of his sky-wide wings still beat shadows
that whisper, *Coulda-coulda-coulda*, as he lights
each dream of prayer awaiting the sun's glow.

TITTERS

Although I couldn't pinpoint
their exact amplitude, I knew
how they sounded: a pitch
lower than a giggle, higher

than a snort, dead-centered
in the smirking glottis.
How I wanted wild creatures
to explode the back wall

where they'd long hidden,
waiting for the right moment
to carry me back into the woods
where I would never speak again.

Living among them, I would learn
to breathe the same as speech.
My eloquent presence would terrify
all. I would stand watch

for the rest of their lives. They would
never have a full night's sleep again.
My breathing would out-loud theirs,
a warning lesson for their children.

ANOTHER GOOD FRIDAY

Oh how many times I'd ached to die:
the question was only how to die.

Should I take apart my father's cheap razors,
slash my wrists, and lie in the tub to die?

Or should I try to climb up the tall chimney
at Norrie School and leap off to die?

Or should I pedal my ten-speed bike
right into an incoming diesel truck and die?

In the end, I swallowed half a bottle of
St. Joseph's orangey aspirins. I didn't die.

I didn't collapse. Just a tummy ache.
I was such a failure! I couldn't even die.

NUMBERS

after Louis Moilanen (1886–1913)

You left Finland for America when you were 4,
homesteading with your parents north of Hancock.
You were tall as any man at the age of 9.

You impressed others with your ability to do
the work of 2 men at the copper mine,
but you couldn't become a miner.
The tunnels were designed for men 5 feet tall.
Your parents were only 5 feet tall.
Where did your height come from?

Then at the age of 19
you were declared the tallest man in the world.

Your shoes were size 19.
Your Stetson hats were size 9.
You were so big that your clothes had to be tailored.
You stood to your full height of 7 foot 9
for the Ringling Brothers and Barnum & Bailey Circus
for 3 years. You stood facing the looks
of shock and amazement at the height of you.
You weren't a man anymore. You were just
designed for enduring endless gawking.
You wanted to head back to the farm
where no one asked the same old questions
about your height, weight, strength.

Yet you passed out your business card
to ladies that said, "Let me see you smile.
Do not spurn me. Looking for
someone to love. Let's get acquainted.
Introduce me to yourself."

How I wanted to sit down with you
far away from the gawkers who stared at my 2 earmolds
popping out like Frankenstein's neck bolts
and lie to you how everything would be all right.

AND SO INTO THE MANY SHROUDS OF NIGHT

I go
when the light glaring into my eyes
slashes my soul
full of melancholic tunes,
and so in despair
I must go.

I know
how to pretend and disguise
that empty hole
in my battered chest festooned
with flowers. Threadbare,
I must flow

to show
that all is fine with their constant lies.
I shall console
myself, as I sleep each moon,
with dreams bright as air.
I'm aglow.

THE PRIESTESS
after Frances "Fran" Peterson (1925–1990)

At my other—and much preferred—church
otherwise known as the Carnegie Library,
I climbed the fourteen steps up to its glass door,
that much closer to Heaven itself.
    I had come to see the priestess herself.

I never paid any attention to the stapled flyers
littering the corkboard on the vestibule's wall.
They were just meaningless fragments
like Father Frank's soft-voiced sermons.
    She aerosoled her bouffant white hair.

Once cocooned inside the nave, I felt safe
from seeing the Dewey card system on my right.
This church was much smaller than St. Michael's.
Its wings were filled with the musk of aging books.
    She easily lit the incense of knowledge.

Its shelves were packed with words and ideas
that would eventually dogma religion right out of me.
The Bible didn't have all the answers, it seemed.
I hadn't known then where else to worship.
    She peered at me over the top of her reading glasses.

The wing on my left housed a tall carrel
of magazines and newspapers, such
hymnbooks that hinted at worlds beyond
the columns of ink that swelled the *Daily Globe*.
    She had the tiniest feet of any woman I knew.

Its pictures stain-glassed my dreams.
It would take years to remove the lead.

No skyscrapers existed in Ironwood.
Its sidewalks didn't bustle with the latest fashions.
Her vestments were swathed in polyester.

In the nave, the three-sided altar winged
piles of returned books, cups of pencils,
a top worn at the edges from so many
books rubbing back and forth for prayer.
She nodded each time I returned the books.

It wasn't just the transaction of dreams
that I wanted when I worshipped there.
She ruled us all with politeness.
Miraculously, she never sermonized.
She knew how to answer my questions.

She knew the shortcuts among the Dewey cards,
even quicker cuts to the exact slot on the shelf.
Each book, found, felt holy in my hands,
a guidebook to worlds outside Heaven.
She never judged what I wanted to check out.

I never learned the story of her life.
She lived across the street from my grandmother.
I never went inside her rectory.
I wanted to tithe my devotion to her.
Everywhere I read, I sit forever in her pew.

THE OTHER WONDER WOMAN

after Lynda Carter playing the eponymous character (1975–1979)

If only I could travel back in time
to stand boldly
smack center of the parking lot
in front of them boys playing Nerf football,
I would take off my earmolds and body hearing aids
(much like how Diana Prince always took off her glasses
and shook her luxuriously long hair free
just before spinning),
and stretch out my arms to spin
(of course never losing my sense of balance
like I tried to spin in the same spot just like her
in the living room late at night
after I'd seen the latest episode)
in an eye-scalding glow
of my nuclear rage radiating
while the beige cords
between my hearing aids and earmolds
turned laser-fire into the Lasso of Truth
suddenly aswirl
with the slickness of neon. Hissing
high above me, the lasso would write-
sear *shame on you* on the undersides
of their eyelids. I would crack it
against the pavement, splintering
their foamy Nerf football into shrapnel
bits of hearing aids stabbing
forever into their girdled souls.

FAR FROM ATLANTIS

In the back of St. Vincent de Paul Store,
    I scoured the latest pile
    of discarded nickel magazines

for unread copies of *Fate* magazine.
    I still hungered to lose myself
    in a world of impossibilities,

desperate to believe
    that I was worthy of grace,
    a little affection.

———

My father brought home a paperback of *Atlantis:*
    The Antediluvian World by Ignatius Donnelly.
    I never knew where he got it.

Maybe it had driftwooded from some island
    balmy with never having to worry about cash.
    But the paperback cost $2.45, which was big money.

I watched his eyes move slowly up and down
    with each wave of page turned, its mysteries
    unfolding in tides ebbing.

———

Question after question colored the lurid headlines
    in my secondhand copies of *Fate*.
    There were no answers, only speculations,

with some insisting that yes, those things did
    happen, ask any witness who was there.
    How I longed to be the recipient of a miracle,

a revelation, incontestable evidence.
    I stared at my hearing aids in the mirror,
    wondering how I could disappear.

———

In the bitterness of winter, he hid by the furnace downstairs
    to read a cheap Western after another, with its covers
    showing men ready with their revolvers.

This book was different. It was thick and stately.
    Its pages were steadfastly white. Was it a Bible
    to a new religion I wasn't supposed to know?

But he was not reading the book downstairs.
    He was reading it right there in the living room
    while us kids babbled around the house.

———

I stole peeks inside its pages, rife with figures
    and charts shoehorned to prove the author's conceit
    that true (white) civilization had emanated from Atlantis.

Mr. Donnelly held forth on the legends and facts,
    quoting at length from various scholars,
    stitching together all sorts of sources

to create a grand picture of the island
    that never was, a place full of bounty,
    blessed with hot and cold springs.

———

One cold evening I was trying to keep warm
    inside his station wagon outside the IGA
    when he unexpectedly plopped a bag of *Fate*

on my lap. He said that someone from St. Vincent's
    had wanted him to give me all the issues for free.
    I skimmed each cover and recognized them.

I said that I'd given those back. I didn't
    need any more. His eyes were
    a Bermuda Triangle of disappointment.

———

In our rare times alone together,
    we never talked about my ears.
    His silences were tacit admissions.

I still dream of us, enrobed in white togas,
    strolling barefoot across the marbled pavement,
    conversing amiably about the world at hand,

just like any father and son would
    with freedom in their eyes, laughing
    at everyone's ridiculous laurel crowns.

THE IRONWOOD EXPERIMENT

Once upon a time I believed my hometown's
landmarks would never evaporate like fog
rushing in to erase everything as if
    never existed,
but they have. St. Michael's Church is now a
parking lot facing the new police station.
The gas station at McLeod and Suffolk has
    been paved over with
asphalt: another parking lot. The building
behind it has vanished into more asphalt.
Pawnshops and thrift stores have proliferated,
    remnants of a town
that doesn't like to recall what it's like now,
preferring a time when mining companies
pulled tonnages of iron ore as if from
    air instead of earth
and loaded them onto trains for ports elsewhere,
making a name for themselves in many war
efforts. Then the earth had nothing left to give.
    The town is a master
illusionist, making big buildings vanish
as if in the blink of an eye. Norrie School,
which took up half a large block, has turned into
    a green carpet of
vacancy, surrounded by houses that still
echo ghost-children who played in recess.
This, here, is the Ironwood Experiment:
    let's see how many
childhood landmarks can be rounded up and tossed
into the Super-Sargasso Sea, a place
where all the lost things go, and where memories
    can be priced for cash.
But the universe isn't any pawnshop.

We're in hock to the mysterious forces
that may or may not honor consignment deals.
    Once it's gone, it's gone,
lingering in our brains' synapses firing
its last breaths of memory trying to save
ourselves from the eventuality of
    this land under sea.

VOICE FROM THE SEA

My voice is a mystery of mangled consonants.
They are slimy stones breaking
                the river of vowels.
They turn into hard
             pimples that never go away.
Go ahead and stone me.

One day this polluted ocean of sickly compliments
will be cleansed. Only then can I
             swim past
the breakwater of hearing aids,
             lined with the larynx's algae.
Spare me the chemical of lye.

Dolphins will accompany me to the end of my days,
bathing me in languages
           I will never know.
I will cast   my first stone. I await
            the first splash of water.

THE ELY STUDENT CENTER, GALLAUDET UNIVERSITY
19 July 1984

Through the sliding doors, I floated
as if plunging into a prism

though I hadn't realized until then
how badly I'd been glassed-in,

stumbling in the wavy darkness
of ignorance woven by those

who'd deemed themselves brilliant
due to their crisp elocution,

only to find the afternoon light
no longer the same tired rainbow

but a solid beam of clarity
cascading through a temple

of glass triangulated above
a pool emptied of water

where waves of transparency rose
and ebbed with unfamiliar faces

while they sat opposite each other
on sofas, eating lunch and laughing

among the potted tall ficus trees
that mirrored in the window looking

into the campus bookstore, swimming
full with textbooks and hoodies.

As I stood by the railing and looked down,
each face cast up a brief welcome at me.

Me, a skeleton who once waited
to die? Could these friendly beings be real?

I had never seen so many signing.
I never knew just how much

I'd hungered for a better religion
until my hands were shorn of speech.

I had no idea that I'd long been wrapped
in a shroud of stars, waiting

for the right supernova to shine.
May this wondrous civilization

never sink. For the first time
I didn't feel the fear of drowning.

I would learn to converse in Water.

THE DAYS OF BRINE

We have always lived underwater.
Our X-ray eyes can pierce the dark blue
where shipwrecks, pocked by mortar,
knit blankets of algae for rescue.
We fashion toys from bones of the drowned.
Sometimes our kids get noisy down
here from banging on splinters. Beware,
we tell them, not to startle the world up there.
It's been thousands of years
since our family breathed air.
The days of brine have no fear.

When our Atlantis began to sink into water,
the officials made a lot of ballyhoo.
They said it was only a temporary matter.
Then Athena, the island's most prized statue,
tipped over into the sea. What a shocking letdown.
All at once our renowned poise left town
as we citizens lurched into a bloody nightmare,
fighting for that last tiny boat. No spares!
Atlantis continued to sink as we rowed clear.
We began to pray to Aer, the god of air:
the days of brine, have no fear!

Friends drifted past like dead fish in the water.
No time for elegies. We had to pull through,
sharing our last few fruits with our daughter
and son. Once blessed with honeydew,
we soon turned mad. We broke down
in hallucination, babbling disjointed nouns,
but our kids seemed not to care.
They continued to kneel in prayer,
and this in spite of the sun's sear!

All they wanted were gills without compare.
The days of brine have no fear.

We thought we'd die of thirst's slaughter
by nightfall. The great Zeus swooped through,
his lightning jolting us right into the water
as our boat caught fire. We turned blue
while flailing against the urge to drown.
Our muscles burned as if in a fiery meltdown.
Exhausted, we surrendered. We didn't care.
Strangely though, we didn't feel scared
as gills began to sprout behind our ears.
We began to shimmer down to anywhere.
The days of brine had no fear.

We've lost track of time in water.
Our bodies have forgotten to age too.
We have no permanent family quarters,
but we must keep moving without ado.
Their sonar waves have tracked us aground.
Soon enough they'll trap us in lockdown,
their cameras snaking around in our lair
and our eyes hurting from the light's glare.
Their contraptions will be without peer,
but surrender we will not declare.
The days of brine have no fear.

In the shadow of their ships, they'll dare
come down in scuba outfits and stare
at us a long time as if to revere.
How could we survive without air?
The days of brine had no fear.

FAR FROM ATLANTIS

THE 29

off the Black River Harbor in July 1976

Lake Superior is trying to boil:
not even a bubble. The lake's surface is a shield.

We strip down to our swimwear anyway.
Our house has no air conditioning.

The shore's lip is clotted with agates
so tiny that they bite our tender soles.

Once in the water, its chill grips our feet.
There's enough clarity to see our toes.

The sky blends down into a blurry horizon.
We imagine seeing Canada.

One by one we drop our young bodies,
tentatively, then with a gasp from the lurch

into the swirling currents underneath,
our bodies awash with its furnaces

churning and pumping fire into our veins.
We soon feel hazy-warm and loose.

I watch my siblings cavort. As the last one
hesitating on the shore, I spot a freighter,

its grasshopper hull the color of rust,
coasting from the west in the far distance.

I am too young to grasp the mechanics
of extracting taconite and transporting it

to other ports where it would be processed
for steel. What I do understand: a ship,

bigger and longer than any I'd seen before,
its white top crossing the horizon.

———

The November before many newspaper headlines
proclaimed the freshly wrecked *Edmund Fitzgerald*,

its 29 men now appearing in
black and white dots, seemingly resigned

to the fate of newsprint and the forgetfulness
of time to come. They were just names to me.

Winter snows came. On my tenth birthday
a hundred ten miles away from home,

I stayed in a large brown house perched above
Houghton and Hancock facing each other,

their boundary defined by the slender crack of water
fleshed out by Lake Superior

twisting through the coppered peninsula.
The Portage Lift Bridge stitched the cities together.

Mornings and afternoons across the bridge,
I imagined catching in the shadows

the frozen bodies of the dead floating
next to the bridge, waiting to be claimed.

The cities seemed painted in gray and white,
the colors of Lake Superior in winter.

On the playground my classmates slow-
motioned like the Six Million Dollar Man.

I wanted the super-strength of those winds
that broke the *Fitzgerald* in half like a pencil.

Spring came with talk of search missions.
Nothing of the 29 turned up.

———

My siblings wave for me to come in, *come in!*
The blood in my ankles curdles from the ice

slaps of water inching upward and forward,
daring me closer to the north. The freighter

continues its course east. I think of ducks
moving without a single bob of head.

I long for webbed feet to paddle me faster,
beyond my siblings laughing among themselves,

circling at full tilt they would spin
like a laundry machine churning in my wake.

Usually a poorly coordinated swimmer,
I would paddle naturally to the freighter.

I am always afraid of swimming pools
but not here. In this lake I would swim like

no one else. Mark Spitz would turn
envious. I'd win more gold medals than him.

A wave slaps up my knees. The sun is
roasting my back, almost a pink onion.

All on the shore must be watching me,
waiting for me to take that fatal plunge.

I take a step forward. The wires of water
noose themselves around my thin thighs.

I try not to think about that awful moment
when the water will clutch madly at my balls.

My skin turns scaly with goose bumps.
I am a fish a-jelly with shivers.

———

Somewhere many hundreds of miles away,
off the Keweenaw Peninsula,

lies the shipwreck of *Edmund Fitzgerald*.
It is a secret no one will decipher.

The newspapers talked of how quickly
that storm on November 10, '75

had materialized out of nowhere.
Couldn't these 29 swim?

After all I had nearly drowned once.
A boy inexplicably shoved me into the deep

of a swimming pool. I tried to shout help,
but I didn't know I had to close my mouth,

timing out each bubble of oxygen.
I flailed. Chlorine nearly filled me.

A pregnant teacher plunged in and rescued me.
I never swam in that swimming pool again.

The lake, waiting, nudges me again.
The cold itches the hems of my swim trunks.

I clam up and squeeze my nostrils shut.
I jump forward. My bloated lungs contract.

The chilly vortex of pebble-dust rising
pummels my stick-body into stiffness.

I'm alive, I think. *I'm still alive!*
My body emanates the sweetest fire.

Melting death right here in this water,
I will rescue those men and their stories.

ACKNOWLEDGMENTS

The author is grateful to the editors of these journals and anthologies for including these poems. (The published pieces from the "In Atlantis" section did not include undercurrent commentaries.)

BlazeVOX: "Island Baby."

Bourgeon Magazine: "Caryatids."

Dispatches from the Poetry Wars: "Another Good Friday" (originally titled "Another Good Friday, When I Was a Teenager").

The Gay & Lesbian Review Worldwide: "Hermes."

Ginosko Literary Journal: "Nessie."

Homology Lit: "Fantastic Archeology: Haibun."

Impossible Archetype: "Poseidon" (originally titled "On Why Poseidon Stopped Creating New Islands") and "Standing before Lake Superior."

Lunch Ticket: "Voice from the Sea."

Nine Mile: "The Deaf Boy from Atlantis" and "Numbers."

Pine Hills Review: "The Archer."

Poetry: "The Six Million Dollar Deaf Boy."

Potomac Review: "Abductions."

Prairie Schooner: "The 29."

Rat's Ass Review: "Ode to the Nuns."

Redefining Disability: An Interdisciplinary Exploration (Paul D.C. Bones, Jessica Smartt Gullion, and Danielle Barber, eds.; Brill): "A Bright Green."

SOFTBLOW: "The Archangel Michael."

The South Carolina Review: "Endlessly in Riverside Cemetery."

The Spark: "Your Bonnet."

Sweeter Voices Still: An LGBTQ Anthology from Middle America (Ryan Schuessler and Kevin Whiteneir Jr., eds.; Belt Publishing): "The Ironwood Experiment."

Walloon Writers Review: "Currents of Ironwood."

We Are Not Your Metaphor: A Disability Poetry Anthology (Zoeglossia Fellows, ed.; Squares & Rebels): "A Prayer to Uri Geller."

Wordgathering: "And So into the Many Shrouds of Night."

———

The poem "Your Bonnet" was the second-place winner for the 2016 Charter Oak Best Historical Writing.

The poem "Caryatids" was nominated for a Pushcart Prize.

———

The author is deeply indebted to Scott Holl for providing such a welcoming space in which to write this book; Eric Norris for his savvy insights with my first pass of *Far from Atlantis* and his utmost patience with its various new poems along the way; David Cummer (*in memoriam*) for his impromptu research on the infamous Philadelphia Experiment; Adam Kauwenberg-Marsnik for the use of his amazing photograph on the cover; Tony Santos (*in memoriam*) for his enduring faith in my work; Mark Ursa for his friendship; Lynne Wiercinski for her assistance in finding a copy of Fran Peterson's obituary; Chael Needle and Tom Steele for their editorial insights; Kathryn Kysar and Andrea Scarpino for their generous words about this book; Katie Lee for her incredible patience and editorial input; and Mary Nichols for having been there for me in ways I cannot begin to explain.

ABOUT THE AUTHOR

Raymond Luczak lost most of his hearing at the age of eight months due to double pneumonia and a high fever, but this was not detected until he was two-and-a-half years old. After all, he was just number seven in a hearing family of nine children growing up in Ironwood, a small mining town in Michigan's Upper Peninsula. Forbidden to sign, he was outfitted with a rechargeable hearing aid and started on speech therapy immediately. Because there were no programs for deaf children in Ironwood, he was brought two hours away to a speech therapy program in Houghton, where he would live with three foster families for a total of nine years, and mainstreamed by himself in Ironwood for five years.

Luczak is the author and editor of over thirty books, including the poetry collections *Chlorophyll, Lunafly,* and *once upon a twin,* which was selected as a Top Ten U.P. Notable Book of the Year for 2021. His prose titles include *A Quiet Foghorn: More Notes from a Deaf Gay Life, From Heart into Art: Interviews with Deaf and Hard of Hearing Artists and Their Allies,* and the award-winning Deaf gay novel *Men with Their Hands.* His work has appeared in *Poetry, Prairie Schooner,* and elsewhere. An inaugural Zoeglossia Poetry Fellow, he lives in Minneapolis, Minnesota.

WHAT IF YOU HAD A TWIN?

"The woods are dark, deep, and quite real in Raymond Luczak's *once upon a twin*. Here, in this dream of a book, the speaker's twin is not miscarried but conjured to comfort the isolated child he was. Through poems describing the speaker's bullying at school and alienation at home where ASL was not a part of family life, the beloved twin becomes a figure for the unnamed, the overlooked, the person who must be restored through love and attention. *once upon a twin* is a fantastic and necessary book." —Connie Voisine, author of *The Bower*

"Hauntingly beautiful. Raymond Luczak has always been a poet of longing, but with *once upon a twin* he has outdone himself. Reaching back as far as his time in his mother's womb, communing with the ghosts that he would grapple with for the rest of his life, he gives us another angle on the Deaf experience. We have much to be grateful for in this epic of story and song." —John Lee Clark, author of *Where I Stand*

A Top Ten U.P. Notable Book of the Year for 2021

Available from Gallaudet University Press in paperback and ebook
ISBN: 978-1-994838-76-8 (paperback)
ISBN: 978-1-944838-77-5 (ebook)